Are Your Mother and Father Related?

by Mrs. Watson's class
with Tony Stead

capstone

Your mother and father are part of the same family.

But are they related? Do they belong to the same group?

Read about different families to find out.

illustrated by Clare

My Family

by Sofia

The people in my family are Mom, Dad, Grandma, and me.

Dad
Grandma
Mom
Me

My Family

by Ethan

The people in my family are Dad, Mom, my brother, and me.

Me
Dad
My brother
Mom

My Family

by Annika

My family likes to walk to the playground near my house.

My Family

by Fiona

My family likes to play games.

Mom

My Family

by Max

My family lives in a big stone house across from my teacher.

My Family

by Tommy

My family lives in a house in Newark.

All our families are different. Some have pets, too!

Our families are the same. They all are part of a group, and they are all related.

This family has a dog for a pet.